D1447941

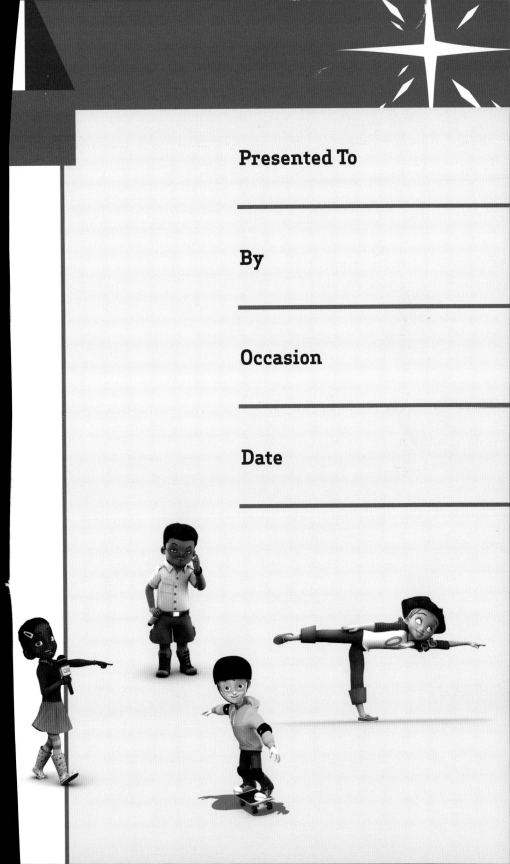

Presented To

By

Occasion

Date

Deep Blue Bible Storybook Christmas

Copyright © 2016 by Abingdon Press.
All rights reserved.

No part of this work may be reproduced or transmitted in any form or by any means, electronic or mechanical, including photocopying and recording, or by any information storage or retrieval system, except as may be expressly permitted by the 1976 Copyright Act or by permission in writing from the publisher. Requests for permission should be submitted in writing to Rights and Permissions, The United Methodist Publishing House, 2222 Rosa L. Parks Blvd., PO Box 280988, Nashville, TN 37228-0988; faxed to 615-749-6128; or submitted via e-mail to permissions@abingdonpress.com.

Scripture quotations are from the Common English Bible. Copyright © 2011 by the Common English Bible. All rights reserved. Used by permission. www.CommonEnglishBible.com.

Co-written by Kerry Blackwood, Daphna Flegal, and Brittany Sky; with special thanks to Elizabeth F. Caldwell
Editor: Brittany Sky
Designer: Matthew Allison

Cover Art (Deep Blue Kids) by: Tim Moen (Character Design), Jesse Griffin (3D Artist), Julio Medina (3D Artist), Eric M. Mikula (Facial Rigging), and Christopher Slavik (Layout Artist);
Background: Four Story Creative.

Internal Art: Four Story Creative; Deep Blue Kids illustrations by Tim Moen, Jesse Griffin, Julio Medina, Eric M. Mikula, and Christopher Slavik.

ISBN: 9781501833151
PACP10501963-01

16 17 18 19 20 21 22 23 24 25—10 9 8 7 6 5 4 3 2 1

Printed in the United States of America

To the Grownups

One of the first songs that children learn in church is "Jesus Loves Me." In this first musical affirmation of faith, they confess that they know that Jesus loves them because the Bible tells them this through stories written across time and cultures. In singing this song and in reading stories about Jesus, a child's spiritual formation begins. But if a child's faith is going to continue to grow with that child, then something more is needed.

Children participate in church educational programs and learn many Bible stories. They possess a lot of factual knowledge about Miriam and Moses, Abraham and Sarah, Ruth and Naomi, David, the stories of Jesus and the people he met, and the beginnings of the church which are told in Acts and the Epistles. Such learning is an important building block in their spiritual formation, and teachers are very important spiritual guides for our children.

But nothing is more important than providing time with a Bible storybook—like this one—engaging children's curiosities about the Bible. Equally essential is the chance for them to ask their own questions about biblical texts, to wonder about the story, to reflect on how they understand and interpret it, and the meaning it has for their lives. This chance for children to engage the Bible with all their curiosity and questions contributes to their development of a language of faith. A child's spiritual formation is as important as her or his growth in the child's abilities as a student, an athlete, a musician, or an artist. And this spiritual formation is incomplete if it only happens in the church. As good as such ministries are, they are insufficient unless supported by parents and families at home.

Children have very important questions about the biblical texts, about the variety of faith expressions they experience in congregations, and about the comments other children make to them, as well as the ones they overhear from adults. As you read Bible stories with children, encourage their questions—the ways they wrestle with the stories they hear. Don't be afraid of questions they ask! Encourage them and join them in this wonderful experience of reading the Bible together. In this way, they won't grow out of it, but rather each time they visit a story, new questions will emerge. It is an incredible spiritual practice that will grow with a child and with you!

Blessings,
Elizabeth F. Caldwell
author of *I Wonder: Engaging a Child's Curiosity about the Bible*

To the Children From the Deep Blue Kids

Hi, friends! We're glad you are here to dive deep with us into God's Word. We'll have adventures and learn fun facts on our journey.

The Bible is more than just a big book; it's a gift to us from God! It's also a gift to us from many people. It took hundreds of years and thousands of people to bring us this gift. And like all good gifts, the Bible is meant to be opened, explored, and enjoyed. It's our hope that you will learn more about God, the Bible, Jesus, faith, and how it all fits into life today.

Contents

Matthew — **1**
Joseph's Story — (Matthew 1:18-24) — 2
Follow the Star — (Matthew 2:1-12) — 4

Luke — **7**
Elizabeth and Zechariah — (Luke 1:5-25) — 8
Gabriel's Message — (Luke 1:26-38) — 12
Mary Visits Elizabeth — (Luke 1:39-66) — 16
Jesus Is Born — (Luke 2:1-7) — 18
Joyous News — (Luke 2:8-20) — 22
Simeon and Anna — (Luke 2:25-31) — 24

Prayers & Songs — **27**
Christmas Songs — 28
Christmas Prayers — 31

Page 34
Learn more about the Deep Blue Bible Storybook

Matthew

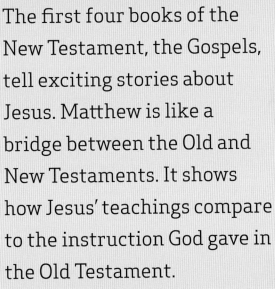

The first four books of the New Testament, the Gospels, tell exciting stories about Jesus. Matthew is like a bridge between the Old and New Testaments. It shows how Jesus' teachings compare to the instruction God gave in the Old Testament.

Tips for **Adults**

The Book of Matthew was written at the end of the first century by an anonymous writer. Church tradition identified the writer as Matthew, but we don't know for sure. We do know that the author teaches the audience that Jesus is the Christ and the interpreter of the Jewish Scriptures. The author teaches us that Jesus came so people could experience God's kingdom.

Joseph's Story
Matthew 1:18-24

In the time before Jesus was born, there was a young man named Joseph. Joseph was engaged to marry a young woman named Mary. Joseph came from the family of King David.

Joseph learned that Mary was going to have a baby. One day Joseph had a dream. In the dream, he saw an angel of God. The angel said, "Joseph, the baby that Mary is having is God's gift to the whole world. Marry her. Name the baby, Jesus, Emmanuel, which means *God with us*."

Joseph did marry Mary. Joseph and Mary obeyed God. When Mary gave birth to a son, Joseph named him Jesus.

Follow the Star
Matthew 2:1-12

At the time when Jesus was born, in a faraway place there were wise men who spent their time watching the stars. One night they noticed a very special star in the sky. It was very bright and seemed to be moving ahead of them. The wise men studied their charts and decided this

special star must be the star that would lead them to the new king.

They wanted to bring special gifts to the new king. They packed frankincense, gold, and myrrh—gifts fit for a king—and set out following the star.

The Book of Matthew was written for a Jewish Christian audience. They would have been shocked that the first people to know about Jesus, the Jewish Messiah, were not Jewish! God's love is big enough for all of us.

The wise men arrived in Bethlehem, following the special star until it stopped over a little house.

When the wise men entered the house, they met the new king, Jesus, and his mom, Mary. The wise men knelt down and offered the new king their gifts of frankincense, gold, and myrrh.

How do you think the wise men felt on their long journey to meet Jesus?

Luke

The Book of Luke teaches us about what Jesus did in the world. Jesus preached the good news, healed people's minds and bodies, and showed everyone he met God's big love. Luke shows us God's love for everyone in the world!

Tips for **Adults**

The author of Luke also wrote the Book of Acts. The author wanted to give an organized narrative account of what happened during Jesus' life and what happened with the first believers to the early Christian groups.

This book explains Jesus' mission in the world. Jesus said he came "to preach good news to the poor, to proclaim release to the prisoners and recovery of sight to the blind, to liberate the oppressed" (Luke 4:18).

Elizabeth and Zechariah
Luke 1:5-25

There was a Jewish priest named Zechariah. He was married to Elizabeth. They were both faithful to God.

Elizabeth and Zechariah wanted to be parents, but they had gotten old. They didn't think they would ever get to have a baby.

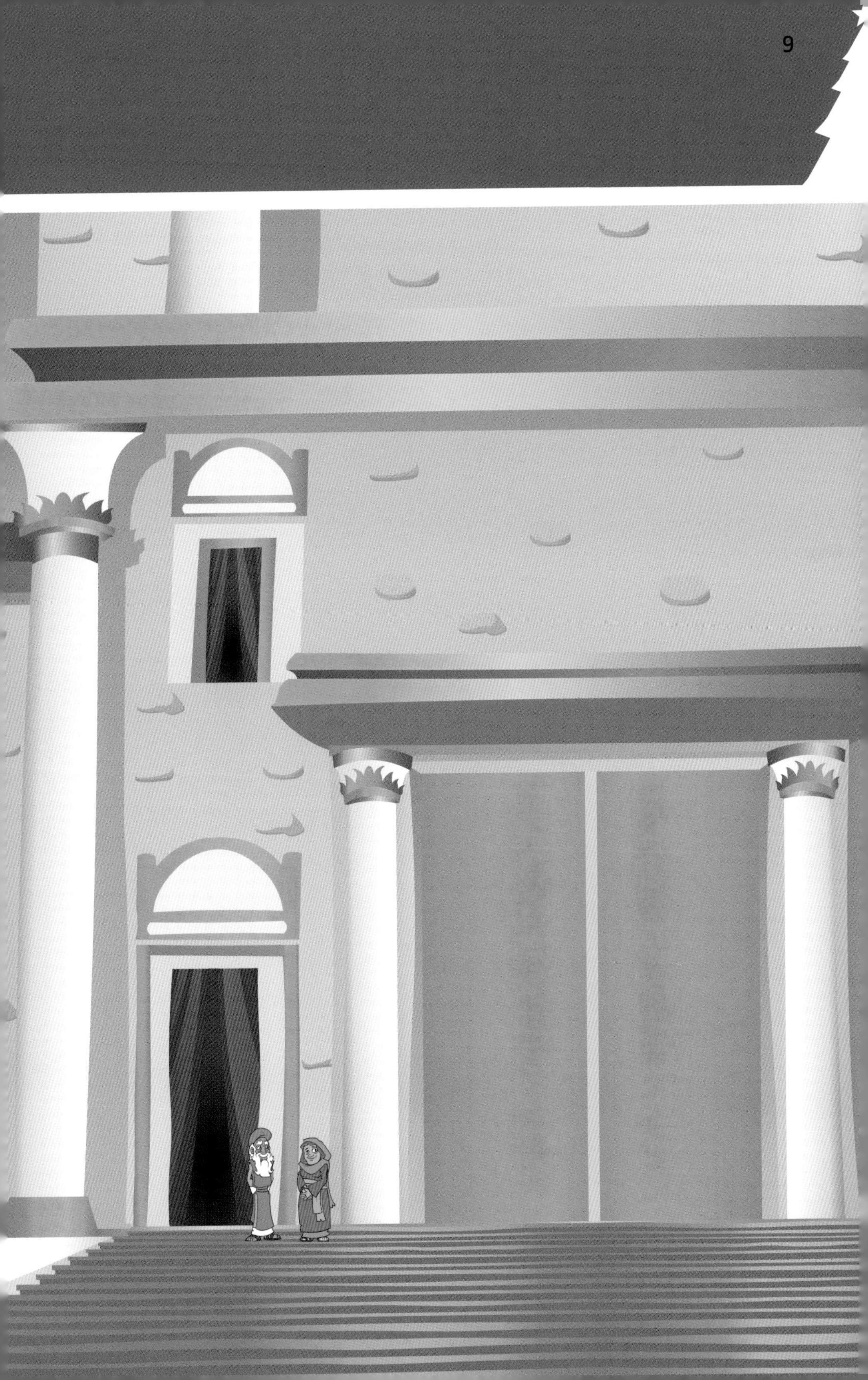

One day Zechariah was working in the Temple. He went into the sanctuary to burn incense. An angel appeared! Zechariah was afraid. The angel said, "Don't be afraid, Zechariah! God has heard your prayers. Elizabeth will have a baby boy."

"You must name him John. He will serve God and help people get ready for the coming Savior."

Zechariah didn't believe the angel because it didn't make sense. He and Elizabeth were too old! "Because you don't believe, Zechariah, you will not be able to talk until John is born."

Zechariah returned home. Elizabeth was pregnant!

What a great blessing! What are some blessings you are happy about?

Gabriel's Message
Luke 1:26-38

Mary lived long ago in the little town of Nazareth. Mary was engaged to be married to Joseph, a carpenter whose family lived in Bethlehem. Mary loved God and did all of the things a young woman was supposed to do.

One day Mary heard a voice. Looking up, she saw an angel standing nearby. At first Mary was frightened!

But the angel Gabriel spoke to her, saying, "Don't be afraid, Mary. God is pleased with you."

Gabriel said, "I have come to tell you good news! God is going to send you a baby boy. You will name him Jesus. He is God's own dear Son, and he is God's greatest gift to the world. He will show everyone how to help one another and how to be happy together."

Mary listened closely to the angel, and her heart was filled with happiness. "I am a servant of God. I will do what God wants me to do," Mary told the angel Gabriel.

How do you think Mary felt in this story?
Do you say yes when God asks you to do big things like Mary?

Mary Visits Elizabeth
Luke 1:39-66

The angel Gabriel had brought good news to Mary—she was going to have a baby boy! Her relative, Elizabeth, was also pregnant. Mary wanted to share the good news about her pregnancy with Elizabeth, so she hurried from her house to Elizabeth's house.

"Elizabeth! Elizabeth! I have good news to share with you!" shouted Mary.

"Wow!" exclaimed Elizabeth. "Mary, as soon as I heard your greeting, my baby leaped for joy! You are very blessed. You are pregnant with God's Son!"

"With all of my heart, I praise God!" sang Mary.

? Mary praised God with singing. How do you like to praise God?

Jesus Is Born
Luke 2:1-7

Mary and Joseph had traveled a long way from Nazareth to Bethlehem. The emperor wanted everyone to go to their hometowns to be counted.

Joseph was from Bethlehem, so he and Mary had to go to Bethlehem. It had been a hard trip—Mary was going to have her baby very soon!

Bethlehem was very crowded and busy. There was no room for Mary and Joseph in the guestroom. That special night, baby Jesus was born. Mary wrapped him in cloth and laid him in a manger.

This is Jesus' birth story. What is your birth story?

Joyous News
Luke 2:8-20

In the fields around Bethlehem, shepherds were watching their sheep.

That night an angel appeared to the shepherds. The angel said, "Do not be afraid. Today in Bethlehem a baby was born for everyone! The baby is God's Son. The baby's name is Jesus! You will find him lying in a manger."

The shepherds said, "Let's go to Bethlehem and see this special baby!"

The shepherds found Mary and Joseph and baby Jesus. They told everyone they saw about the new baby.

The shepherds praised God for letting them see the special baby Jesus.

? How do you think the shepherds felt that night?

Simeon and Anna
Luke 2:25-38

It was a very special day for baby Jesus. Joseph and Mary were taking Jesus to the Temple for the first time. Jesus was going to be dedicated to God at the Temple.

Simeon watched as the young family came inside God's Temple. Simeon was very old and loved God very much.

He walked over to Mary and Joseph, and asked if he could hold Jesus. "This is all I have lived for," said Simeon. "A long time ago, God promised me that I would live long enough to see the Messiah, and here he is!" Simeon was so happy, he sang a song of praise and thanksgiving to God.

Just then, an old woman approached the group gathered around baby Jesus. Her name was Anna. Anna was an old prophetess. She saw Jesus' face and declared that Jesus was the Messiah to all who could hear. She praised God for the Messiah, just like Simeon.

How do you like to praise God when good things happen?

Prayers & Songs

Prayer is talking to God. Praying can be silent, quiet, or loud. Prayer can be done through anything—singing, dancing, walking, or even playing. You can pray for yourself and for other people.

Tips for
Adults

The following pages are filled with songs and prayers. Invite the children to sing and pray along with you. The rhythms, music, words, and meaning will stick with your children for their whole lives.

Christmas Songs

Sleep, Baby Jesus
(Tune: Rock-a-Bye, Baby)

Sleep, baby Jesus,
sleep on the hay.
Mary is singing.
Little lambs play.
Joseph is watching
stars shine so bright.
So sleep, baby Jesus,
sleep through the night.

A Child Has Been Born for Us
(Tune: Mary Had a Little Lamb)

A child has been born for us, born for us,
born for us.
A child has been born for us. He is the
Son of God.

Shining Star
(Tune: This Old Man)

Shining star, shining star,
shine to show us where you are.
Shine your light on little Bethlehem;
guide the path of the wise men.

Name Him Jesus
(Tune: Did You Ever See a Lassie?)

You will name the baby Jesus,
the angel told Mary.
You will name the baby Jesus,
for he is God's Son.

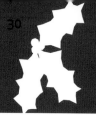

Three Wise Men

(Tune: Twinkle, Twinkle, Little Star)

Twinkle, twinkle, shining star.
We are wise men from afar,
following a star so bright,
looking for a king this night.
Twinkle, twinkle, shining star.
We are wise men from afar.

Christmas Prayers

A Christmas Thank-you Litany
by Sharilyn S. Adair

Here is the stable where Jesus was born—
Thank you, God, for baby Jesus.

a cow and a donkey keep him warm,
Thank you, God, for baby Jesus.

Joseph and Mary to take care of him,
Thank you, God, for baby Jesus.

and a warm manger bed to lay him in.
Thank you, God, for baby Jesus.

Here is the baby, asleep in the hay—
Thank you, God, for baby Jesus.

a gift of God's love both then and today.
Thank you, God, for baby Jesus.

Good News! Clap! Clap!

by Elizabeth Crocker

Good news! Clap! Clap!
(Clap hands twice.)
Good news! Tap! Tap!
(Stomp feet twice.)
Christmas Day is near.
*(Make a C with your right hand. Move the C
in an arc in front of your body. This is sign
language for Christmas.)*

Good news! Clap! Clap!
(Clap hands twice.)
Good news! Tap! Tap!
(Stomp feet twice.)
Listen to me cheer!
(Cup hands around mouth.)

Good news! Clap! Clap!
(Clap hands twice.)
Good news! Tap! Tap!
(Stomp feet twice.)
Mary has a son.
(Pretend to rock baby Jesus in your arms.)

Good news! Clap! Clap!
(Clap hands twice.)
Good news! Tap! Tap!
(Stomp feet twice.)
God loves us, every one.
(Hug yourself.)

Deep Blue Bible Storybook

Do you want even more great Bible stories?

Some of your church's very youngest children can understand the Bible with the help of the *Deep Blue Bible Storybook*. Written in language children ages 3 to 6 can understand, it includes 146 stories that will help your children learn the books of the Bible and practice beginning Bible skills. Children love the *Deep Blue* curriculum characters that are featured in the book and will look forward to learning prayers and fun songs set to familiar tunes with their *Deep Blue* friends.

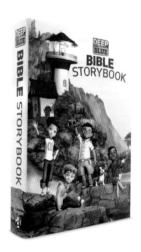

Learn more at *deepbluekids.com*.